Mastering Crypto Trading

For

Beginners

The Essential Beginners Guide to Mastering Cryptocurrency Trading and Investment Strategies to Daily Profit

Gideon Flynn

Copyright © [2024] [Gideon Flynn]

No part of this book may be reproduced, stored in a retrieval system, or transmitted in any form or by any means, electronic, mechanical, photocopying, recording, or otherwise, without the prior written permission of the publisher.

Table of contents

Introduction 8
   Embarking on the Crypto Adventure: A Beginner's Guide. 8
CHAPTER ONE 10
   Crypto Exchanges: The Gateway to Trading 10
   Basic Trading Strategies 12
CHAPTER TWO 14
   Analysis of Trading Volumes and Market Capitalization 14
   News and Events: The Response of the Market 16
CHAPTER THREE 18
   Day Trading: The Exhilaration of the Quick Chase 18
   Swing Trading: The Art of Medium-Term Navigation 19
   Long-Term Investing: The Patient Treasure Hunter's Approach 19
   Risk Management: The Essential Survival Kit 20
CHAPTER FOUR 22
   Chart Patterns: The Secret Language of the Market 22
   Trend Lines and Support/Resistance: The Cartographer's Tools 23
   Indicators and Oscillators: The Trader's Dashboard 23
   Advanced Chart Patterns: The Expert's Playbook 24
CHAPTER FIVE 26
   Blockchain Technology: The Foundation of Crypto 26
   Financial Metrics: The Crypto Investigator's Toolkit 27
   Market Dynamics: The Crypto Ecosystem 27
   On-Chain and Off-Chain Analysis: The Crypto Detective's Guide 28
CHAPTER SIX 30
   Wallet Security: The Treasure Chest of Safety 30
   Phishing and Scams: The Pirate's Playbook 31
   Trading Psychology: The Mind Games of the Market 31
CHAPTER SEVEN 34
   Trend Following: The Art of Riding the Wave 34
   Range Trading: The Strategy of Patience 35
   Breakout Trading: The Art of Catching the Wave 35
   Scalping: The Fast-Paced World of High-Frequency Trading 36

CHAPTER EIGHT...38
    Diversification: The Key to Risk Management........................ 38
    Asset Allocation: The Science of Portfolio Optimization........ 39
    Risk Management: The Art of Protecting Your Portfolio..........40
    Performance Measurement: The Metrics of Success........... 40
CHAPTER NINE...42
    The Thrill of the Win: The Euphoria of Profit........................... 42
    The Agony of Defeat: Coping with Loss..................................42
    Fear and Greed: The Twin Enemies of Trading..................... 43
    The Importance of Mindfulness and Self-Care.......................43
CHAPTER TEN... 46
    The Rise of Decentralized Finance (DeFi).............................. 46
    The Growing Importance of Regulation.................................. 46
    The Evolution of Trading Platforms and Tools........................47
    The Expanding Universe of Cryptocurrencies........................47
CONCLUSION...48

ACKNOWLEDGEMENTS

As we embark on this journey through the realm of cryptocurrency trading, we stand on the shoulders of giants. We're grateful for the collective wisdom, innovative spirit, and unwavering support of the following individuals and communities:

- The pioneers of blockchain and cryptocurrency, who dared to dream of a decentralized future
- Our fellow traders and investors, who share their insights and experiences, fueling our growth and learning
- The open-source community, whose tireless efforts have created powerful tools and resources
- Our loved ones, who patiently endure our late-night research sessions and enthusiastic ramblings about crypto
- Our team of editors, designers, and proofreaders, who refine our work with precision and dedication.

WHAT TO KNOW

As you dive into this guide, keep in mind:

- Cryptocurrency trading carries risks and uncertainties; always do your own research and never invest more than you can afford to lose
- The market is constantly evolving; stay informed, adapt, and be prepared for unexpected twists and turns
- This guide is meant to be a starting point, not a definitive resource; seek out diverse perspectives and continue learning
- The cryptocurrency community is a powerful force; engage with others, share your knowledge, and contribute to the growth of this vibrant ecosystem.

With gratitude and excitement, we share this guide with you. May it serve as a valuable companion on your crypto trading journey!.

PREFACE

"Embarking on a journey through the realm of cryptocurrency trading can be a thrilling adventure, but it can also be a daunting maze to navigate. As a beginner, you're likely to encounter a cacophony of conflicting opinions, bewildering terminology, and hair-raising market fluctuations. But fear not! This guide is your trusted compass, designed to steer you through the uncharted territories of crypto trading and empower you to make informed decisions that will propel you towards financial freedom.

Within these pages, we'll delve into the mysteries of blockchain and cryptocurrency, unravel the enigmas of technical analysis, and demystify the art of risk management. Our aim is to transform you from a curious novice into a confident crypto trader, equipped with the knowledge, skills, and intuition to thrive in this dynamic market. So, buckle up and join us on this exhilarating journey into the world of cryptocurrency trading!"

Introduction

Embarking on the Crypto Adventure: A Beginner's Guide

Welcome to the captivating world of cryptocurrency trading, where financial freedom and innovation converge! As a beginner, venturing into this uncharted territory can be both exhilarating and intimidating. With the crypto market's vast potential and rapid evolution, it's essential to have a reliable guide to navigate the complexities and unlock success.

This comprehensive guide is designed to be your trusted companion on the crypto trading journey. We'll delve into the fundamental concepts, demystify the jargon, and provide a solid foundation for your adventure. From the basics of blockchain technology to advanced trading strategies, we'll explore the exciting world of crypto trading together.

With the right knowledge and mindset, you'll be empowered to make informed decisions, avoid common pitfalls, and capitalize on the vast opportunities the crypto market offers. So, let's embark on this thrilling adventure together and uncover the secrets of successful crypto trading!

"Embrace uncertainty, for it is the fertile ground where growth and innovation flourish."

&

Remember, uncertainty is a natural part of life and growth. Instead of fearing it, learn to embrace it and use it as an opportunity to learn, adapt, and thrive!

CHAPTER ONE

Charting Your Course

As you begin your crypto trading journey, it's essential to understand the landscape of exchanges, trading platforms, and basic trading strategies. In this chapter, we'll delve into the world of crypto exchanges, exploring the different types, their features, and how to choose the right one for your needs.

Crypto Exchanges: The Gateway to Trading

The core of the cryptocurrency trading ecosystem is made up of cryptocurrency exchanges, which give buyers and sellers a place to trade cryptocurrencies. With so many exchanges accessible, it's important to know the various kinds and what makes them special.

- **Centralized Exchanges (CEXs):** These exchanges function similarly to conventional stock exchanges, with user funds being held in a central authority that oversees transactions.

- **Decentralized exchanges, or DEXs:** Using blockchain technology, DEXs facilitate peer-to-peer trades decentralized from a central authority.

- **Hybrid Exchanges:** These combine the advantages of DEXs and CEXs.

When choosing an exchange, take into account elements like:

- **Security:** Seek out exchanges that have strong security features, like cold storage and two-factor authentication.
- **Fees**: Recognize the various charge structures, such as those for trading, deposits, and withdrawals.
- **User Interface:** Select an exchange that best fits your trading style based on its user-friendly interface.
- **Currency Support:** Verify that the exchange accepts the digital currencies you wish to transact with.

Putting Your Trading Platform in Place

After selecting an exchange, the next step is to configure your trading platform. We'll walk you through each step, going over:

- **Account Creation:** Creating an account and confirming it.
- Implementing two-factor authentication and creating a strong password are examples of security measures.
- **Deposit and Withdraw:** Transferring money into and out of your account.
- **Interface Navigation:** Getting to know the interface of the exchange and personalizing your dashboard.

Basic Trading Strategies

As a beginner, it's crucial to build a solid foundation in basic trading strategies to avoid common pitfalls and set yourself up for success. Think of these strategies as your trading toolbox - with the right tools, you'll be empowered to make informed decisions and navigate the markets with confidence.

Buying and Selling: The Art of Execution

Buying and selling are the most fundamental actions in trading, but it's surprising how many beginners get it wrong. Understanding market orders and limit orders is key to executing your trades effectively.

- *Market Orders*: Imagine shouting "I'll take it now!" - a market order buys or sells at the current market price, no questions asked.

- *Limit Orders*: Think of it as saying "I'll take it at this price or better" - a limit order buys or sells at a specific price you set, giving you control over your entry and exit points.

Market Analysis: Reading the Charts

Market analysis is like trying to solve a puzzle - you need to understand the pieces to see the bigger picture. Basic chart analysis helps you identify trends, patterns, and potential trading opportunities.

- **Trends:** Identify the direction of the market (up, down, or sideways) to make informed trading decisions.

- **Chart Patterns:** Recognize common patterns like triangles, wedges, and reversals to anticipate potential price movements.

Risk Management: Protecting Your Portfolio

Risk management is like having an insurance policy - it helps you minimize losses and maximize gains. Setting stop-losses and managing your portfolio is crucial to trading success.

- **Stop-Losses:** Set a "panic button" to automatically sell if the price drops below a certain level, limiting your potential losses.

- **Portfolio Management:** Diversify your trades, set position sizes, and monitor your overall exposure to minimize risk and optimize returns.

By mastering these basic trading strategies, you'll be well on your way to trading like a pro! Remember, trading is a journey, and continuous learning is key to success.

CHAPTER TWO

Decoding Market Dynamics

As you venture deeper into the crypto market, understanding the intricacies of market dynamics becomes crucial. In this chapter, we'll delve into the world of market analysis, exploring the forces that shape the crypto landscape.

Analysis of Trading Volumes and Market Capitalization

Consider the market capitalization and trading volume of a cryptocurrency as the heart and soul of the market, similar to the rhythm section of a band!

Capitalization of the Market: The Drumbeat

Providing the fundamental beat of the market, market capitalization functions similarly to a drumbeat. When the entire supply is multiplied by the current price, the total worth of all coins in circulation is determined. An desirable cryptocurrency for traders and investors is one with a high market capitalization, or a strong drumbeat, which denotes stability and liquidity.

Valuing Exchanges: The Bottom Line

The trading volumes of the market provide vitality and depth to its rhythm, just like the bass line does. They show the total quantity of coins that have been traded in a given period of time (e.g., 24 hours). High trade volumes, or a strong bass line, suggest the liquidity and market activity of a cryptocurrency, which facilitates buying and selling.

Unity and Discord

The market is stable and in balance when trading volumes and market capitalization are in balance. Discord between the two, however, may point to possible problems:

A cryptocurrency's susceptibility to price manipulation may be indicated by its low market capitalization and large trading volumes.
Low trade volumes and a high market capitalization could be signs of inactivity and liquidity in the market.

In Harmony with the Marketplace

You can become more aware of the rhythm of the market and more capable of making well-informed trading judgments by studying market capitalization and trade volumes. Recall that while a powerful bass line and drum rhythm can help your trading approach, they cannot ensure success.

Chart Analysis 101: Recognizing Patterns and Trends

The cartographer's tool for navigating the cryptocurrency market is a chart. We'll acquaint you with technical analysis by investigating:

- **Candlestick charts:** A visual representation of market mood and price action.
- **Trend lines and support/resistance:** recognizing trends and forecasting changes in price.
- **Indicators and Oscillators:** Interpreting Sentiment and Market Momentum

News and Events: The Response of the Market

Consider the bitcoin market as a dynamic, constantly-evolving puzzle. Events and news are like the jigsaw pieces that continuously change and reconfigure the scene in the market. Keeping up with the most recent developments (news and events) and comprehending how they fit into the larger scheme (market trends and patterns) are essential to solving the puzzle.

The News Feed: Keeping Up to Date

Consider events and news as a never-ending news feed that is always changing and impacting the market. To maintain your lead, you must:

- Set up alerts for news and events that could move the market. - Pay attention to reliable sources and cryptocurrency news portals.

- Keep up with international political and economic trends. The Response of the Market: Examining the Tea Leaves

The market may respond to news and events in ways that are not predictable. In order to comprehend the reaction of the market, you must:

- Examine the impact of news and events on market patterns and trends.
- Determine the attitude and feelings of the market
- Understand how certain events and news affect different cryptocurrencies.

With confidence, you can now solve the riddle and decide which trades to make."

By the time this chapter is out, you'll have the knowledge and skills necessary to assess market dynamics, choose wisely when trading, and confidently traverse the cryptocurrency landscape.

CHAPTER THREE

Trading Strategies for Treasure Hunters

To traverse the ups and downs of the cryptocurrency market, as a treasure hunter, you need a map. We'll look at a number of trade techniques in this chapter to assist you in finding your prize.

Day Trading: The Exhilaration of the Quick Chase

Day trading is like the adrenaline rush of the trading world. It's all about buying and selling assets, like coins, within the same trading day. One of the biggest advantages is the potential for quick profits. Traders can capitalize on short-term price movements and make multiple trades in a single day.

However, day trading also comes with its fair share of challenges. It requires a lot of time and attention since you're constantly monitoring the market for opportunities. It's fast-paced and can be emotionally draining, especially during volatile market conditions.

To navigate this frenzy, day traders rely heavily on charts and technical indicators. These tools help them identify trends, support, and resistance levels, which are crucial for spotting profitable deals. Risk management is key in day trading. Traders use techniques like setting stop-loss orders to limit potential losses and ensure they don't get caught in a downward spiral.

Swing Trading: The Art of Medium-Term Navigation

Swing trading strikes a balance between the quick pace of day trading and the long-term perspective of investing. Traders hold onto assets for a few days to weeks, aiming to profit from short to medium-term price fluctuations.

One advantage of swing trading is that it allows traders to capture larger price movements compared to day trading. They look for trends and patterns in the market, using technical analysis to identify entry and exit points.

Like any strategy, swing trading has its pros and cons. It requires less time and attention than day trading but still demands a good understanding of market dynamics. Managing risk is crucial, and traders often use techniques like setting stop-loss orders and diversifying their portfolio to minimize losses.

Long-Term Investing: The Patient Treasure Hunter's Approach

Long-term investing is like the slow and steady race. It involves holding onto assets for an extended period, usually months to years, with the goal of significant appreciation over time.

The main advantage of long-term investing is the potential for substantial returns, especially if you invest in promising assets early on. It requires patience and a strong belief in the fundamentals of the assets you're holding.

However, long-term investing also comes with risks, such as market volatility and potential downturns. Investors need to conduct thorough research to identify promising coins and build a diversified portfolio to spread risk.

Risk Management: The Essential Survival Kit

Regardless of the trading strategy, risk management is the cornerstone of success in the financial markets. It involves techniques and practices aimed at protecting capital and maximizing returns.

Setting stop-loss orders is a common risk management technique across all trading strategies. It helps limit potential losses by automatically selling an asset if it reaches a certain price level. Diversification is another key aspect, spreading investments across different assets to reduce overall risk exposure.

Position sizing and risk-reward ratios are also vital. Traders and investors determine how much capital to allocate to each trade or investment based on their risk tolerance and potential reward.

In summary, each trading strategy offers unique opportunities and challenges, and mastering risk management is crucial for navigating the complex world of trading and investing.

Observations & Reviews

CHAPTER FOUR

Technical Analysis for Crypto Cartographers

Technical analysis is like deciphering the hidden code of price movements in the cryptocurrency market. It involves using charts and indicators to predict future trends based on historical price data. Let's explore the key components of technical analysis and how they apply to crypto trading.

Chart Patterns: The Secret Language of the Market

Imagine chart patterns as the unique vocabulary of the market, each pattern telling a story about potential price movements. Common patterns include head and shoulders, triangles, and wedges. By learning to identify and interpret these patterns, traders can gain insights into market psychology and anticipate possible price directions.

For example, a head and shoulders pattern typically indicates a trend reversal, while triangles suggest a period of consolidation before a potential breakout or breakdown. Understanding the psychology behind these patterns helps traders make informed decisions about when to enter or exit trades.

Trend Lines and Support/Resistance: The Cartographer's Tools

Trend lines act as maps, guiding traders through the market terrain. They are drawn by connecting significant highs or lows on a price chart, indicating the direction of the trend. Support and resistance levels, on the other hand, represent key price levels where buying or selling pressure is expected to emerge.

Traders use trend lines to gauge the strength and direction of trends, while support and resistance levels help identify potential entry and exit points. Breaking through a resistance level could signal a bullish trend, while breaching support might indicate a bearish trend.

Indicators and Oscillators: The Trader's Dashboard

Think of indicators and oscillators as the instruments on a trader's dashboard, providing valuable insights into market sentiment and momentum. Moving averages, such as the Simple Moving Average (SMA) and Exponential Moving Average (EMA), help smooth out price fluctuations and identify trend directions.

The Relative Strength Index (RSI) and other oscillators measure the speed and change of price movements, indicating whether an asset is overbought or oversold. Traders use these indicators to confirm trading signals and make informed decisions about when to enter or exit trades.

Advanced Chart Patterns: The Expert's Playbook

Advanced chart patterns are like the masterstrokes in a trader's playbook, requiring a deeper understanding of market dynamics. Patterns like wedges, triangles, cups, and handles are more complex but can offer valuable insights into future price movements.

By mastering advanced chart patterns, traders can anticipate major market shifts and position themselves strategically to capitalize on potential opportunities. Understanding the underlying psychology behind these patterns is key to unlocking their predictive power.

In conclusion, technical analysis empowers crypto traders to navigate the market with confidence, leveraging chart patterns, trend lines, indicators, and advanced strategies to make informed trading decisions. Mastering these tools is essential for becoming a successful crypto cartographer.

"Manage emotions during trading. Stay calm, avoid greed or fear-driven decisions, and maintain a clear, logical mindset for effective trading."

CHAPTER FIVE

Fundamental Analysis for Crypto Investigators

Fundamental analysis is like peering into the DNA of a cryptocurrency to understand its true value. It goes beyond price charts and technical indicators, focusing on factors such as blockchain technology, financial metrics, market dynamics, and both on-chain and off-chain data.

Blockchain Technology: The Foundation of Crypto

At the core of every cryptocurrency is blockchain technology, a decentralized and immutable ledger. Understanding blockchain architecture, consensus mechanisms (like Proof of Work or Proof of Stake), and security measures is crucial for assessing a cryptocurrency's reliability and potential for scalability.

Analyzing blockchain metrics such as transaction volume, block time (the time it takes to mine a new block), and network activity provides insights into the underlying infrastructure's efficiency and usability.

Financial Metrics: The Crypto Investigator's Toolkit

Financial metrics offer a snapshot of a cryptocurrency's economic health and market position. Market capitalization, calculated by multiplying the coin's price by its total supply, gives an indication of its overall value and market dominance compared to other cryptocurrencies.

Trading volumes and liquidity measures reveal the level of activity and market interest in a particular cryptocurrency. Evaluating financial statements, if available, can provide insights into revenue streams, expenses, and profit margins, akin to analyzing traditional company financials.

Market Dynamics: The Crypto Ecosystem

The crypto market is a dynamic ecosystem influenced by various factors. Identifying and analyzing market trends, sentiment (positive or negative attitudes towards a coin), and overall market conditions helps investors make informed decisions.

Understanding the different players in the market, from individual retail traders to institutional investors and influential whales who hold large amounts of cryptocurrency, helps gauge market sentiment and potential price movements. Market volatility, the degree of price fluctuations, is also a critical factor to consider when assessing risk and potential returns.

On-Chain and Off-Chain Analysis: The Crypto Detective's Guide

On-chain analysis involves examining blockchain data directly, such as transaction history, wallet addresses, and network activity. This data provides insights into user behavior, network congestion, and adoption rates.

Off-chain factors, including news events, social media sentiment, regulatory developments, and industry trends, also play a significant role in shaping cryptocurrency prices. Combining on-chain and off-chain analysis offers a comprehensive view of a cryptocurrency's overall health and potential future performance.

By mastering fundamental analysis techniques and delving deep into the underlying factors that drive cryptocurrency value, crypto investigators can make more informed investment decisions and navigate the dynamic crypto landscape with confidence.

you'll have a solid understanding of fundamental analysis and its applications in crypto trading in this chapter, enabling you to make informed investment decisions and navigate the market with confidence.

"Patience is key; don't rush into trades. Wait for favorable opportunities, and avoid emotional decisions that can lead to losses."

CHAPTER SIX

Navigating Risk and Security in Crypto Trading

Crypto trading comes with its share of risks, but understanding and implementing proper risk management and security measures are essential for a safe and successful crypto journey.

Wallet Security: The Treasure Chest of Safety

Your crypto wallet is like a treasure chest, holding your digital assets. Understanding the different types of wallets, such as hot wallets (connected to the internet), cold wallets (offline storage), and hardware wallets (physical devices), is crucial for choosing the right one based on your security needs.

Setting up and securing your wallet involves using strong passwords, enabling two-factor authentication (2FA), and storing backup phrases securely. Best practices for wallet management include regular updates, avoiding sharing sensitive information, and using reputable wallet providers.

Phishing and Scams: The Pirate's Playbook

Being able to identify and avoid phishing attempts, such as suspicious emails or websites asking for your private keys or login credentials, is essential for protecting your assets.

Recognizing common scams, like Ponzi schemes or fake ICOs (Initial Coin Offerings), and reporting them to relevant authorities or platforms helps protect the crypto community. Protecting yourself from social engineering attacks, where attackers manipulate you into revealing sensitive information, requires vigilance and skepticism.

Trading Psychology: The Mind Games of the Market

Trading psychology is like navigating the mind games of the market. Understanding market emotions and sentiment, such as fear, greed, and euphoria, helps you make rational decisions amidst market fluctuations.

Managing emotions like fear of missing out (FOMO) or panic selling during market downturns is crucial for long-term success. Developing a disciplined and patient mindset, setting realistic goals, and sticking to your trading plan can help you avoid impulsive decisions based on emotions.

Portfolio Management: The Treasure Hunter's Diversification Strategy

Diversification is the treasure hunter's strategy for managing risk. Understanding portfolio management involves spreading your investments across different assets (diversification) to reduce overall risk exposure.

Allocating assets based on your risk tolerance, investment goals, and market conditions is key to optimizing your portfolio. Regularly rebalancing and adjusting your portfolio ensures it stays aligned with your investment strategy and risk management goals.

By mastering risk management techniques, securing your assets, understanding trading psychology, and implementing a diversified portfolio strategy, you can navigate the challenges of crypto trading with confidence and resilience.

"Only invest what you can afford to lose. Avoid overleveraging or risking funds needed for essential expenses, ensuring financial stability."

CHAPTER SEVEN

Mastering Crypto Trading Strategies

In this chapter, we'll explore advanced crypto trading strategies designed to help you navigate the market with precision and confidence, aiming to maximize profits while minimizing losses.

Trend Following: The Art of Riding the Wave

Trend following is like catching a wave in surfing, aiming to capitalize on established market trends. It involves identifying and aligning with the prevailing direction of the market. Understanding trend analysis involves studying price charts, identifying key support and resistance levels, and using technical indicators like moving averages to confirm trends.

Traders use indicators such as the Moving Average Convergence Divergence (MACD) or the Average Directional Index (ADX) to confirm trend strength and momentum. Managing risk in trend following involves setting stop-loss orders to protect profits and using trailing stops to ride the trend while locking in gains.

Range Trading: The Strategy of Patience

Range trading is akin to navigating within the boundaries of price ranges. It involves identifying areas of support and resistance where prices tend to oscillate. Traders wait for the price to reach these levels and then enter trades, aiming to profit from price bounces within the range.

Understanding range trading involves patience and discipline, waiting for clear signals of price reversals at support or resistance levels. Technical indicators like the Relative Strength Index (RSI) or Bollinger Bands can help identify overbought or oversold conditions within a range.

Managing risk in range trading involves setting tight stop-loss orders outside the range boundaries and taking profits when the price approaches the opposite range boundary.

Breakout Trading: The Art of Catching the Wave

Breakout trading is like seizing opportunities when the market breaks out of established price ranges. It involves identifying and capitalizing on significant price movements that signal a breakout from consolidation phases.

Understanding breakout analysis involves monitoring chart patterns such as triangles, rectangles, or flags that indicate potential breakouts. Traders use volume analysis, momentum indicators like the Moving Average Convergence Divergence (MACD), and chart patterns to confirm breakout signals.

Managing risk in breakout trading involves setting stop-loss orders below or above breakout levels, depending on the direction of the breakout, and using trailing stops to protect profits as the price continues to move in the breakout direction.

Scalping: The Fast-Paced World of High-Frequency Trading

Scalping is like sprinting in the fast-paced world of trading, aiming to make quick profits from small price movements. It involves executing multiple trades within short timeframes, typically seconds to minutes.

Understanding scalping requires speed, precision, and access to real-time market data. Scalpers rely on technical indicators like moving averages, stochastic oscillators, or order flow analysis to identify short-term price fluctuations and capitalize on them.

Managing risk in scalping involves using tight stop-loss orders and having a strict risk-reward ratio to ensure that winning trades outweigh losing ones, given the high frequency of trades.

By mastering these advanced crypto trading strategies and implementing robust risk management techniques, traders can navigate the market with agility and exploit various market conditions to their advantage.

CHAPTER EIGHT

The Art of Crypto Portfolio Management

Effective portfolio management is like orchestrating a symphony, balancing risk and reward to achieve long-term success in crypto trading. Let's explore the strategies and techniques that can help you manage your crypto portfolio like a pro.

Diversification: The Key to Risk Management

Diversification is the cornerstone of portfolio management, akin to spreading your investments across different instruments to reduce risk exposure. Understanding diversification involves recognizing its benefits, such as reducing overall portfolio volatility and increasing potential returns by tapping into different market sectors.

Creating a diversified crypto portfolio involves allocating funds to various cryptocurrencies, tokens, and assets with different risk profiles, market caps, and use cases. This helps mitigate the impact of negative price movements in any single asset on your overall portfolio.

Managing risk through diversification involves regularly assessing your portfolio's composition, rebalancing if needed, and staying informed about market trends and developments across different sectors.

Asset Allocation: The Science of Portfolio Optimization

Asset allocation is like fine-tuning an engine, optimizing your portfolio's performance by allocating percentages of your capital to different asset classes based on risk and return objectives. Understanding asset allocation involves recognizing its importance in achieving a balance between growth and stability.

Creating an optimal asset allocation strategy involves assessing your risk tolerance, investment goals, and time horizon. For example, allocating a portion of your portfolio to stablecoins or less volatile assets can provide stability during market downturns, while allocating another portion to high-growth assets can boost long-term returns.

Rebalancing and adjusting your portfolio periodically ensure that your asset allocation remains aligned with your investment strategy. This may involve selling overperforming assets to take profits and reallocating funds to underperforming assets to maintain balance and optimize returns.

Risk Management: The Art of Protecting Your Portfolio

Risk management is like putting up shields to protect your portfolio from potential threats. Understanding risk management involves acknowledging its importance in preserving capital and minimizing losses during market fluctuations.

Identifying and managing risks in your portfolio involves assessing various factors such as market volatility, liquidity, regulatory changes, and cybersecurity risks. Using tools like stop-loss orders, which automatically sell assets if they reach predetermined price levels, and position sizing, which determines how much capital to allocate to each trade based on risk, helps manage risk effectively.

Performance Measurement: The Metrics of Success

Performance measurement is like taking stock of your progress, evaluating your portfolio's performance against predefined benchmarks and goals. Understanding performance measurement involves recognizing its importance in assessing the effectiveness of your investment strategy.

Using metrics such as Return on Investment (ROI), which measures the profitability of your investments relative to their cost, and the Sharpe Ratio, which assesses risk-adjusted returns, helps evaluate performance objectively. Adjusting your strategy based on performance data involves learning from successes and failures, making informed decisions, and continuously refining your portfolio management approach.

By mastering the art of crypto portfolio management, including diversification, asset allocation, risk management, and performance measurement, you can navigate the volatile crypto markets with confidence and build a resilient and profitable portfolio over time.

CHAPTER NINE

The Emotional Rollercoaster of Crypto Trading

Crypto trading is a thrilling journey filled with emotional highs and lows that can impact your mental and emotional well-being. Understanding and managing these emotions is crucial for maintaining a balanced and resilient mindset.

The Thrill of the Win: The Euphoria of Profit

Winning trades can evoke feelings of euphoria and excitement. However, it's essential to stay grounded and avoid letting emotions cloud your judgment. Recognizing the effects of euphoria on your trading decisions helps maintain discipline and make rational choices.

Strategies for managing the thrill of the win include practicing humility, maintaining perspective, and avoiding impulsive decisions driven solely by emotional highs. Celebrate successes but remain focused on long-term goals and risk management.

The Agony of Defeat: Coping with Loss

Losses are inevitable in trading and can be emotionally challenging. Coping with loss involves acknowledging the emotional impact, allowing yourself to process feelings of disappointment or frustration, and reframing losses as learning experiences rather than failures.

Strategies for coping with loss include maintaining a resilient mindset, practicing self-compassion, and implementing risk management techniques such as stop-loss orders. Bouncing back from losses involves staying resilient, learning from mistakes, and staying committed to your trading strategy.

Fear and Greed: The Twin Enemies of Trading

Fear and greed are common emotions that can influence trading decisions. Fear of missing out (FOMO) or fear of losses can lead to impulsive actions, while greed can drive excessive risk-taking.

Managing fear and greed requires self-awareness, discipline, and a well-defined trading plan. Strategies for managing these emotions include setting realistic goals, sticking to your trading strategy, and avoiding emotional reactions to market fluctuations.

The Importance of Mindfulness and Self-Care

Mindfulness and self-care are essential for maintaining emotional balance and well-being in crypto trading. Practicing mindfulness helps you stay present, focused, and aware of your emotions without being controlled by them.

Incorporating mindfulness techniques such as meditation, breathing exercises, and mental visualization into your trading routine can help reduce stress, improve decision-making, and enhance overall resilience. Prioritizing self-care, including exercise, healthy eating, and adequate rest, supports mental and emotional health during trading.

By acknowledging and managing the emotional aspects of crypto trading, cultivating mindfulness, practicing self-care, and staying disciplined in your trading approach, you can navigate the emotional rollercoaster with resilience and confidence.

Observations & Reviews

CHAPTER TEN

The Future of Crypto Trading

As we peer into the future of crypto trading, we witness a landscape filled with innovation, challenges, and opportunities that will continue to reshape the way we trade and invest in cryptocurrencies.

The Rise of Decentralized Finance (DeFi)

Decentralized Finance (DeFi) is at the forefront of revolutionizing traditional finance and trading. It encompasses a range of financial services and applications built on blockchain technology, including lending, borrowing, trading, and asset management.

The emergence of DeFi brings forth the potential to democratize access to financial services, eliminate intermediaries, and provide greater financial inclusion globally. However, it also presents challenges such as smart contract risks, regulatory uncertainties, and scalability issues that traders and investors need to navigate.

The Growing Importance of Regulation

As crypto trading gains mainstream adoption, regulatory frameworks are becoming increasingly crucial. Governments and regulatory bodies worldwide are grappling with how to classify and regulate cryptocurrencies, exchanges, and related activities.

The benefits of regulation include investor protection, market stability, and legitimacy, which can attract institutional investors and foster greater trust in the crypto ecosystem. However, regulatory compliance also brings challenges such as compliance costs, legal complexities, and potential constraints on innovation.

The Evolution of Trading Platforms and Tools

Trading platforms and tools continue to evolve to meet the evolving needs of traders and investors. Advanced trading platforms offer features such as algorithmic trading, customizable charting tools, and automated portfolio management.

The rise of social trading and copy trading platforms allows traders to connect, share insights, and replicate successful strategies. Additionally, advancements in artificial intelligence (AI) and machine learning (ML) are enhancing trading analytics, risk management, and decision-making processes.

The Expanding Universe of Cryptocurrencies

The cryptocurrency market continues to expand with new tokens and projects entering the scene. These new cryptocurrencies offer diverse use cases, ranging from decentralized applications (dApps) to non-fungible tokens (NFTs), and innovative blockchain solutions.

Navigating this expanding universe of cryptocurrencies requires thorough research, due diligence, and risk management strategies. Traders and investors must stay informed about market trends, project fundamentals, and regulatory developments to make informed decisions in this dynamic and ever-changing landscape.

The future of crypto trading is brimming with potential, driven by innovations like DeFi, evolving regulatory landscapes, advanced trading platforms, and a diverse array of cryptocurrencies. By staying adaptable, informed, and strategic, traders and investors can navigate the complexities and seize opportunities in this exciting frontier of finance and technology.

"*Define clear trading goals and strategies. Stick to your plan, avoid impulsive actions, and maintain discipline for consistent results.*"

CONCLUSION

And that concludes our captivating journey through the world of crypto trading, a realm brimming with excitement, challenges, and boundless opportunities. As we bid adieu to these pages filled with insights and knowledge, let us carry forward the essence of what we've learned.

Crypto trading, much like an exhilarating adventure, beckons us with promises of discovery and growth. It's a landscape where knowledge, skills, and emotional resilience intertwine, shaping our path to success.

Remember, each trade is not just a transaction but a step toward mastering the art of trading. Stay curious, for the crypto realm is ever-evolving, offering new horizons and possibilities waiting to be explored.

In this vast universe of crypto, where risks and rewards dance in harmony, it's essential to embrace a mindset of continuous learning and adaptability. With every challenge comes an opportunity, and with every setback, a chance to learn and grow stronger.

As we close this chapter, let us reflect on the words of wisdom that guide us: "The future belongs to the bold, the prepared, and the resilient."

May your journey in the crypto realm be filled with wisdom gained, wonders discovered, and wealth amassed through diligence and perseverance. Let us navigate this decentralized frontier together, creating our own narratives and painting our futures with brilliance and purpose.

Farewell, fellow traveler, may your adventures in crypto trading be as rewarding as they are enlightening. Here's to a future where each trade is a stroke of brilliance on the canvas of our success!

Until we meet again, happy trading, and may fortune favor the bold!

Please support us in dropping an honest review particularly on this book in other to reach out to more people looking for a book like this, and as well to also improve customer service experience .

HAPPY TRADING!

"Celebrate successful trades but learn from losses. Analyze both wins and setbacks to refine your strategy and improve future trading outcomes."

19-DAY TRADING PLAN

Days	Reviews	Remarks
1		
2		
3		
4		
5		
6		
7		

8		
9		
10		
11		
12		
13		
14		
15		
16		

17		
18		
19		

www.ingramcontent.com/pod-product-compliance
Lightning Source LLC
Chambersburg PA
CBHW071221240526
45470CB00018B/2099